FARM ANIMALS

Horses

by Emily K. Green

BELLWETHER MEDIA · MINNEAPOLIS, MN

Note to Librarians, Teachers, and Parents:

Blastoff! Readers are carefully developed by literacy experts and combine standards-based content with developmentally appropriate text.

Level 1 provides the most support through repetition of high-frequency words, light text, predictable sentence patterns, and strong visual support.

Level 2 offers early readers a bit more challenge through varied simple sentences, increased text load, and less repetition of high-frequency words.

Level 3 advances early-fluent readers toward fluency through increased text and concept load, less reliance on visuals, longer sentences, and more literary language.

Whichever book is right for your reader, Blastoff! Readers are the perfect books to build confidence and encourage a love of reading that will last a lifetime!

This edition first published in 2007 by Bellwether Media.

No part of this publication may be reproduced in whole or in part without written permission of the publisher. For information regarding permission, write to Bellwether Media Inc., Attention: Permissions Department, Post Office Box 1C, Minnetonka, MN 55345-9998.

Library of Congress Cataloging-in-Publication Data
Green, Emily K., 1966–
  Horses / by Emily K. Green.
     p. cm. — (Blastoff! readers. Farm animals)
Summary: "A basic introduction to horses and how they live on the farm. Simple text and full color photographs. Developed by literacy experts for students in kindergarten through third grade"—Provided by publisher.
  Includes bibliographical references and index.
  ISBN-13: 978-1-60014-067-9 (hardcover : alk. paper)
  ISBN-10: 1-60014-067-X (hardcover : alk. paper)
  1. Horses—Juvenile literature. I. Title.

SF302.G72 2007
636.1—dc22   2006035306

409 068 5

Contents

Many farms
have horses.

A horse can help with farm work. These horses pull a wagon.

This brown horse
helps move the cows.

A horse eats grass.
A horse can **graze**
for many hours
each day.

A horse also eats **grains**, **hay**, apples and carrots.

13

A horse has a tail. A horse swats flies with its tail.

tail

A horse has a **mane** on its neck and head.

mane

A horse can be
a good **pet**. This
owner **grooms**
his horse every day.

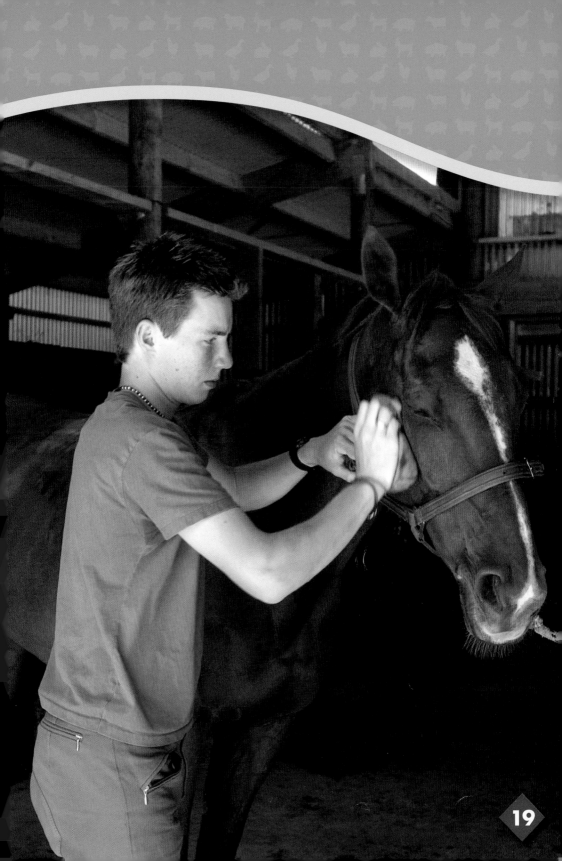

19

Many people ride horses for fun. Do you like horses?

Glossary

grains—the seeds of cereal plants like wheat or oats

graze—to eat grass growing in an open field; horses can eat and walk at the same time.

groom—to clean and brush an animal

hay—grass or other plants that are cut, dried, and fed to animals

mane—the long hair that grows from the head and neck of a horse

pet—an animal that you keep and take care of for fun

To Learn More

AT THE LIBRARY

Gibbons, Gail. *Horses*! New York: Holiday House, 2003.

Meister, Cari. *My Pony Jack*. New York: Viking, 2005.

Peterson, Cris. *Horsepower: The Wonder of Draft Horses*. Honesdale, Penn.: Boyds Mills Press, 1997.

Silverman, Erica. *Cowgirl Kate and Cocoa*. Orlando, Fla.: Harcourt Children's Books, 2005.

ON THE WEB

Learning more about farm animals is as easy as 1, 2, 3.

1. Go to www.factsurfer.com

2. Enter "farm animals" into search box.

3. Click the "Surf" button and you will see a list of related web sites.

With factsurfer.com, finding more information is just a click away.

Index

The photographs in this book are reproduced through the courtesy of: Cathleen Clapper, front cover; Cindy Haggerty, p. 5; Andre Jenny/Alamy, p. 7; Ted Wood/Getty Images, p. 9; Johner/Getty Images, p. 11; blickwinkel/Alamy, p. 13; Karen Givens, p. 15; Cathleen Clapper, p. 17; Tim Graham/Alamy, p. 19; Trout55, p. 21.